Husband of a Praying Wife

Written by Minister Lisa Harris

ISBN 9798423817763

Kindle Direct Publishing

www.kdp.amazon.com/en_US

Cover Design: Ivan D. Ursery II/Evangelistic Designer
ivandurseryII@gmail.com

Editor: Julie Helliwell
juliehelliwell@live.com

Dedication

I dedicate this book to my heavenly Father, who inspired me to write this book for Him. Except for His speaking to me during an experience of high praise and worship, revealing to me that He needed me to write this book; it would have never been written.

Acknowledgments

As I begin my story, I give thanks to my Heavenly Father, who inspired me to share my life and His blessings in the pages of this book. He gave me the intention of drawing my readers closer to Him and, more specifically, bringing married couples closer to each other. I am honored to share pieces of my story with you within these pages, hoping and praying that your marriages may become all that Father God has ordained for your lives. Marriage is honorable. His word proclaims, "The two of you shall be as one flesh."

I thank you, Father God, for assisting me in this venture, for this truly could not be written without Your insight. I pray that You will restore marriages across the nations by way of the knowledge I have gained through You, which is now being revealed in this book.

Thank you, Jerome Harris, my husband, and closest friend, for giving me the freedom to tell our story to all who will read it. Thank you for assisting me in writing portions from a husband's perspective and revealing your thoughts. Thank you for trusting me to write this book and for your love and support. I love you; our love shall endure forever.

I'd like to thank Patrice, my firstborn daughter, for all of your assistance in writing this book. You are the writer of the family, and I hope that this book will inspire you to write a book of poetry, unveiling to the world a part of your creativity. You are so precious to me. I love you more and more each day. Your beauty shows forth in everything you do. After three years of marriage desiring to have children, God gave us His best, you. What joy you give to us.

The Bible Scripture, Exodus 20:12 (NKJV), which reads, "Honor your father and your mother," brings me to thank you, Mother, my beautiful queen. You taught me many of life's values that I uphold today, including how to love and respect all people. You have always been there for me, a wonderful, caring support system throughout the years. You also honor my husband, Jerome.

Mother happens to be a single woman who raised three beautiful children on her own. I will always be proud of her and grateful for all that she instilled in me and my sisters as we grew up. Even now, I am thankful for all the love and time we share together.

Thank you, Aerial, my youngest daughter and friend, for all of the love and encouragement you have shown me during this book-writing endeavor. I appreciate and love you dearly for providing your time to help type and assist when needed. What a great treasure you are to me.

I also thank my son, Minister Timothy, for all of your assistance and words of knowledge during this process. Truly you are a special blessing to our family and to the body of Christ. I love you, son.

Contents

Preface

Many of us can recall the times when we were reminded by mom, dad, aunts, uncles, and friends of the family what a beautiful baby we were. Usually, around the time my birthday would be nearing, or on my birthday, my mother would talk about events that occurred on the day that I was born. Mom said, "What a beautiful and adorable baby girl you were. Plump, pretty, and perfect." Mom would make bows of ribbon and attach them to my head, finding a way to make them adhere since I had no hair at birth. She often excitedly reminisced that on the day I arrived home from the hospital, there had been a snowstorm. "Days after you were born, your dad and I brought you home, and there was so much snow, we could barely enter the door with you. It looked like a blizzard outside!"

As months went by, during the many times when I would cry, Mom said that all she had to do was to turn on the music, and the tears would go away. As a little girl, I enjoyed listening to music. While I was still in her womb, Mom said she would often place a book on her abdomen and read to me. What a great influence this had on me! Even now, I enjoy reading books and listening to the comforting sounds of music!

Then there was my great-granddaddy, Bishop LaSalle Clark, who greatly influenced my current life through his prayers for me before my life even began by laying hands on my mother's pregnant abdomen! Mother said that he prayed for a safe and healthy delivery without complications and that she and I would have a long life together. It happened just as my great-granddaddy prayed it would. Mother gave birth to a healthy baby girl named Lisa Marie Welch.

Thank God for all of those prayers, which gave me strength, mercy, and grace. Bringing me to my teenage years, I recall being alone in my bedroom, lying in my bed in complete silence, daydreaming about how I desired to attend college. My mother was a single parent during that time, and I felt that if I attended college, I could obtain a degree in an area of study in which I could have financial abundance to help her out.

During my freshman year, my grades were fair. I could have done much better if I had focused and studied harder, but my sophomore year was different. Focusing more on wanting to get accepted into college one day caused me to become more disciplined with my studies. My grades then went to a higher level on the grading scale.

In the year of 1979, I graduated from high school. A few weeks later, it was time to go off to college, and Indiana University Bloomington was my destiny! Along with many other students throughout the cities of Indiana, I was in a summer program called "Groups." This program allowed high school graduates to attend college early, receiving credits before the freshman school year began. What a blessing it was to be a part of this program. In addition to accumulating credits early on, it allowed us to become familiar with the campus buildings as well as meet new friends before the fall semester began.

During my freshman year on a college break, I came home and found that my great-granddaddy, Bishop LaSalle Clark from Memphis, Tennessee, was visiting my Grandma Mavis here at home. I happened to be dating Jerome at that time, and he joined me, Mother, and my two sisters on a visit to see them. Upon meeting Jerome, Great-Granddaddy thought very highly of him, wanting to perform our wedding ceremony that same day! Of course, Jerome and I were not ready for that. Not yet!

Everyone dreams of that fairy tale moment when they meet their Prince Charming (of course Jerome), fall even more deeply in love, get married, and ride off into the sunset; happy now and forever! Unfortunately, getting to that forever point is not so simple. Imagine thinking you have everything that you ever wanted, including the perfect doting husband who loves and cherishes you for who you are and ever dreamed of being; him being a best friend, marriage partner, head money maker, and confidant. However, in the blink of an eye, after being married for 11 years, the relationship with the person who knew you the best shatters. Most everything you both wanted and agreed upon has changed.

Now you find yourself residing in the same home but living different lives, no longer united together. You wake up asking yourself, "Who is this man that I married, and how did I even get here?" Do you just lay down in defeat and give up, or do you fight for your marriage and purpose in what God has planned for your life?

"This Is My Story"

To every woman and every man who found the Lord before your spouse did, I want you to know that you are not alone. The purpose of this book is to let married couples with unbelieving husbands or wives and married couples with problems know that whatever they are going through in their marital relationship, God has the power to fix, heal, and restore. You do not have to give up on your marriage when your relationship has gone awry (wrong). HOLD ON!

You can choose to fight for it.

CHAPTER 1

Finding Love

Jerome Harris was born to wonderful parents, Mamie (Peaches) and James Harris. Jerome grew up in a strong Baptist, Christian-based home. He had three siblings: two older brothers and one younger sister; all were raised by their parents with much love and structure. They awakened early each morning to a hearty breakfast before walking to school. When school was out, they came home to an ample dinner prepared by their mother, followed by completion of homework and daily chores, then playtime. The kitchen closed at a certain time. When the streetlights came on, they had better be within their mother's view. If rules were not followed, including being in the house on time, there would certainly be consequences to follow.

In spite of strict rules, there was much love, and Jerome, his brothers, and his sister had a lot of fun growing up. They had many friends in the neighborhood, and the boys played quite rough with one another, as most boys did. Their sister Cindy was much younger than they were and therefore did not play much with her brothers. Jerome, his brothers, and friends built ramps and did dangerous challenges such as jumping from them on their bikes, seeing who could jump the farthest. As a result of this, their bikes would often need to be rebuilt or repaired. At times, they would take bike rides that took them to many places throughout the city before making it home in time for supper.

During summer breaks and on the weekends, Jerome's dad, James Harris, a ceramic tile setter in Chicago, Illinois, and other suburban areas, would take him, along with his brothers, to help complete jobs. James would pay them well, according to their ability. These young men were trained at an early age to become professional ceramic tile setters and received a valuable lesson about working hard then being rewarded for it. They were members of the Tile Setters Union. The business was owned by their father, who named it Harris Tile.
During Jerome's high school years, he attended The Career Center in Gary, Indiana. The welding trade was his field of study. After graduating high school, he received his credentials and began working for the United States Steel Corporation as an apprentice welder. After three years in the apprentice program, he became a coded welder at United States Steel Mill. After two years of graduating high school, Jerome met the love of his life, me, Lisa. After dating for a few years, Jerome asks for Lisa's hand in marriage.

Now let me tell you some background knowledge about the perfect woman for Jerome.

I, Lisa Marie Harris, was born to Evelyn and Nolan Welch, a very young married couple. Mom was sixteen, and my dad was seventeen years old when they got married. She became pregnant with me at seventeen. They were both brought up in Christian homes. My grandma on my dads' side of the family was a righteous woman, as was my grandma on my mothers' side. Therefore, I was raised in a home filled with love and unity. I was taught what was proper and improper at a very early age. Living a sheltered life of my own choosing, as a child, I did not go out to play much. I enjoyed reading books and watching television, catching up on my favorite shows, and playing with my dolls.

As I reached my early teens, I recall my two sisters, my mother, and I would visit my grandmother every week after church service. We would also visit her midweek. Most times, I would rather stay home alone to do homework, chores, and watch television. On the contrary, my sisters enjoyed playing with their friends outside, playing kickball, riding a bicycle, and doing all the fun things that children normally do.

One summer day, while at home, I happened to be lying across my bed taking a nap. My bedroom door was open, and my mother called out to me, "Come here, Lisa."

I woke up and immediately went into the living room area where they were.

She said, "I have someone I would like you to meet. This is James's son, Jerome."

James, a tile setter and member of our church, came by with his son to fix the bathroom floor. I had no idea that such a handsome, distinguished young man would ever cross my path. After the introduction, Jerome and I went our separate ways. Later that evening, I received a call from him inviting me to a movie. After conversing on the phone for quite some time, my response was yes. It occurred to me that since my mother and his dad were friends, it would be perfectly fine to go to the movies with him. It turned out to be such an innocent date; there was no kissing or anything of the kind. Although Jerome did try to hold my hand, I immediately pulled back from him. After the movie was over, Jerome was a gentleman and took me home. We stayed in contact with each other and became friends.

The years seemed to fly by. During my high school years, I knew that I desired to attend college. That was when I studied my hardest to get the best grades possible, knowing this would enable me to be accepted to my college of choice.

Before I knew it, graduation day was approaching. What a great, wonderful day it was. Caps and gowns, golden tassels, tears of joy and sorrow, wondering when we will see our friends again. Not to mention three weeks later, I was to travel to Indiana University Bloomington, Indiana, to attend a summer program called "Groups." This program helped me to receive credits for some of my prerequisites before the fall program began.

Months later, Jerome and I dated while I was in college. Jerome would visit me about every other weekend, and he had come to visit during the 'Big Ten weekend' game. During this weekend visit, there was much elation in the air, and to add to the excitement, Jerome asked me to marry him. We had already had a glorious celebration because Indiana University Bloomington college had just won the Big Ten: men's basketball game. Once the game and all the celebrating was over, Jerome walked me back to my dorm, Brisco. He walked me upstairs to my room hallway to say our goodbyes. While in the hallway, he told me how much he loved me. He looked straight into my eyes and said, "I love you so much, Lisa; I can't live without you in my life. Will you marry me?" I replied, "Yes!" We were so happy and bubbling over with joy - what an awesome time in our lives.

Friendship was important, but now we were engaged. We were inseparable. We did everything together. We began to trust one another more and more. Jerome would wine and dine me, taking me to some of the most elegant restaurants to eat. He would take me to the movie theater and theater shows in the Chicago area. We would go to the beach and watch the sunset. We went for picnics in the park. He swept me off my feet. Jerome always tried to make me happy.

After the semester was completed, we decided that I would come home. I did return home to live with my beautiful mother. I call her beautiful because she taught me to have great values and how to treat people with love and respect.
While living with her, I obtained a job as a cashier. This position enabled me to save money to assist in the planning and payment of our wedding. As time went by, Jerome and I realized that it was time to inform our parents of our plans to get married.

One sunny day, my mother was in a great mood. She was happy and filled with joy that day. I thought this was the perfect time to tell her the exciting news.
I said, "Ma, Jerome and I plan to get married next year."
She asked, "Why don't you wait a while before getting married?"
I replied, "Well, we are waiting a whole year."
Mom then gave us her blessing.

Jerome told me that his dad was home one morning, and he asked if there was time to talk with him.

His father replied, "Yes."

Jerome then said, "I have met the woman of my dreams."

His dad replied, "One of the most important things you will ever do in your life is to pick the right woman to marry. It is a major responsibility. Once you make that decision, it should be for life. This type of decision cannot be overturned without repercussions. Children could become involved later."

Jerome stated, "She is the one."

James totally agreed. He was happy about Jerome and I deciding to come together in marriage. Jerome and his dad began to discuss some details concerning wedding dates and necessities.

As time passed by, Jerome and I began to get more serious about one another. We knew we wanted to spend our lives together forever. Wedding vows meant that we would love, protect, honor, and cherish each other 'until death us do part.' Jerome and I began to talk about the things we both thought would enhance our wedding ceremony.

Planning our Wedding

Although it took approximately a year to plan our wedding, it was wonderfully exhilarating. We were blessed to have an excellent wedding planner who kept everything organized. She happened to be a member of our church, Liberty Baptist. James Harris, Jerome's father, helped to build our church and later became an active member. He served on the Board of Trustees as well as on the Usher Board. Jerome grew up there as a child and sang in the choir. However, he was not in attendance much after he became an adult. My family and I later became members; therefore, we still have sentimental values connected to this glorious house of God. Even today, it is a beautiful church filled with loving and caring members. It was tremendously befitting that we would have our wedding there with the many precious memories we shared and such a remarkably beautiful edifice for the occasion!

Our first moments of excitement were those generated at our rehearsal dinner, held in a room beautifully decorated in burgundy and white. The colors blossomed as love and joy filled the air. I presented each of my five bridesmaids, maid of honor, and our flower girl with lovely, wrapped gift boxes containing a gold necklace with matching earrings. The necklaces and earrings sparkled with several diamond stones set in them. Everyone seemed to be pleased with their gifts.

Jerome had seven groomsmen, two men to light the forty candles of the candelabra, and his ring bearer. The evening drew late, so we all said our farewells to go home and prepare for the big day. Everyone was so excited awaiting tomorrow.

When tomorrow came, it was our wedding day! My mother, wearing a gorgeous pink formal dress, drove me to church. As I finished getting dressed, looking at me with delight, she pulled out a lovely flower bouquet just for me. I was so touched and loved her so much for being here by my side. She supported me, and not just for now. All of my life, she had been there for me, right up to this very moment!

The day was glorious, including the weather. Our special day, October 30, 1982, was amazingly unbelievable and perfect for a wedding with such a warm, bright, and sunny sky. No snow, no rain, just clear blue heavens.

Jerome stood there at the altar so astonishingly handsome, his groomsmen by his side and two of them lighting the lovely candelabra. It was such a beautiful sight to behold, intensified by my five bridesmaids, each wearing white baby's breath in their hair and long, gently flowing dresses of burgundy and white, slightly draping off of their shoulders. My maid of honor wore a pale pink long, gently flowing dress, slightly draping off her shoulders. She also had white baby's breath in her hair.

My wedding dress was white with puffy sleeves called Pronovias or Juliet-style sleeves. Draping slightly off my shoulders, it was gorgeous. The material was made of silk, long and flowing with a flare of softness at the bottom. My veil was a white floral headpiece of tulle, flowing gently past my thighs. The train was simply breathtaking; it had concealed buttons, which transformed into a royal bustle. The dress then became evening wear for the reception. And what a stunning bouquet I held, consisting of white carnations and burgundy-colored roses.

Much time was spent on planning and anticipation, and although the wedding began and ended within approximately 45 minutes, it was truly "heaven right here on earth." What a wonderful wedding it was. We received so many raving comments of enjoyment and approval from our guests. I must say, it was a magical experience for me.

We both enjoyed conversing, hearing well wishes, and congratulations. After the wedding was over, there was time to take pictures at the church and to relax before arriving at our exquisite wedding reception. As I thought of the stunning bridesmaids, maid of honor, and the elegance of the ceremony, I thought of Jerome's eyes as he looked into mine;

we both knew we would be united forever, in unity. Mark 10:8 says, "and the two are united into one." (NLT)

Upon arriving at our wedding reception, we were pleased with how everything was so beautifully and professionally arranged. Our grand entrance was graciously applauded as we entered the ballroom where the reception was being held. Everything was of pure excellence, including the food, which was catered by our grand chef, a dear friend of the family.

Friends and family presented us with a vast array of gifts, including not only beautifully wrapped presents but also hefty monetary gifts that helped sustain us through the winter. No one would have known that, during this time, Jerome was laid off from the US Steel Mill. With our gifts, stored up savings for the wedding reception, my cashier job's salary, and the Lord's help, we were never lacking.

After leaving the wedding reception, Jerome and I got into our car, decorated with balloons, paper streamers, and our "Just married" sign on the back, and drove to our elegant hotel. Jerome not only graciously drove me there but upon arrival at our hotel room, he also picked me up and lovingly carried me over the threshold to start our new life together. We were very happy and so much in love.

Trust

When two individuals decide to come together in marriage to one another, there are two great components needed in the union. Love and trust are important attributes to a blessed relationship. Joy overflows in them when they become one in unity. Jerome had great plans for our life together. His number one goal is to keep me safe. As his wife, I have always trusted Jerome to keep me safe.

Another important component needed in marriage is communication. Once the children were added to our family unit, Jerome consistently ensured that our safety remained intact. He would call home daily from work to communicate and to make sure our family were in the house and that at a certain time, things were locked up. We would talk about our day and how the children were doing. It is always important to talk to one another on a consistent basis. It will strengthen your relationship and allow you to have an even greater friendship.

Communication also builds trust. It causes one to have a greater cohesiveness in your relationship. Trust is one of the main factors in every positive and healthy relationship. I find that the more you trust and your partner trusts, the stronger the relationship becomes.

CHAPTER 2

Marital Happiness and Joy

After the honeymoon was over, we both returned to work. Our normal weekdays consisted of coming home from work and honoring my husband Jerome by preparing dinner for him. During our earlier years of marriage, Jerome assisted his dad as a ceramic tile setter. Jerome and his dad worked in Chicago, Illinois, so he would return home between the hours of five or six o'clock in the evening. I worked at a grocery store as a cashier.

Jerome and I worked together in our home. We both made sure that the daily chores were taken care of. I basically cared for the inside-of-the-house duties, and Jerome took care of the outside of our home. I folded the laundry; he washed the clothes. Never did I have to iron his pants and shirts; he faithfully took them to the cleaners to be cleaned, starched, and pressed.

Jerome shared with me how he made a promise to the Lord that "if He would allow me to be his wife, he would treat me like a queen." So, Jerome never put pressure on me to cook or clean. Of course, I did cook and clean. We just enjoyed one another and our life together. We never had problems with money or problems with paying our bills. Jerome gave me the money consistently. He would say, "That is not my money Lisa, it doesn't belong to me; this is our bill money." I would be responsible for making sure that the checks were sent to the various businesses.

Shortly after a month of being married, we visited our in-laws. My middle sister, Brenda, lived in Wisconsin at that time. We would visit her from time to time. On our weekends, we would often travel, doing mostly short, 2-to-3-hour trips. We enjoyed going to different locations. We weren't as busy with our lives then; there were no children yet, during this time.

During our second year of marriage, Jerome and I flew to Nassau, Bahamas! What a beautiful island paradise! Perfect for lovers! We spent a lot of time on the beach since our hotel was surrounded by it. Although the Bahamas is popular for diving and snorkeling, we did not take advantage of those water sports. One thing I remember so vividly was that we did enjoy the boat excursion. We got on this large boat, and the floor was made of clear glass. We were able to see the beautiful coral reef beneath. The fish were so colorful! We saw all kinds of exotic fish and sea creatures approaching. Later we stopped for lunch. As the evening was nearing, we decided to take a little walk. While walking, we explored the shopping markets to purchase souvenirs. What a glorious week we had there, and an awesome way to cap off our second year of marriage!

Yes, our visit to the Bahamas was a joy of a lifetime, but still, there was the joy of returning home, seeing and visiting friends and family again. Upon returning home, Jerome and I spent some quality time with them before the start of a new working week. Mostly during Monday through Fridays, we were enjoying our own home. After dinner, we might watch a movie together, play a game, or spend some time talking and sharing with one another. We'd later prepare for the next day before going to bed. Many times our weekends were filled with family gatherings, birthday parties, weddings, anniversary parties, and celebrations. Jerome and I would always attend events together. We were inseparable! I must say that this was our life! Fun-filled and delightful!

Entering into our second year of marriage, many family and friends began to ask about children.
"Are you going to have children?" they would ask. "When are you planning to have a baby?"
We began to respond, "When it happens, it will happen."
We continued to have fun-filled days, laughter, and communication. Oftentimes we would explore Chicago, Illinois. We would attend car shows, the taste of Chicago, the Shedd aquarium, concerts, and many other enjoyable sites.

Then the third year came. I began to feel different. My body was changing. My stomach felt bloated as if it had extra air in it, not to mention breast changes, including tenderness and swelling. I talked to Jerome about it, and he said, "Make sure you don't do too much. Don't exercise too much, take it easy," speaking as if he knew before I did that I was pregnant.

As time passed, I thought, 'Let me make an appointment to see a doctor.'
So the appointment was made, and the doctor gave me the news that we were going to have a baby! Upon sharing the news with Jerome, he was so excited! He even picked me up and swung me around with so much joy, happiness, and enthusiasm that it was igniting! Soon followed the morning sickness, the bland diet, the tea and crackers, clear sodas, and water. All in all, it was worth everything that we had to go through during early pregnancy.

In preparation for the baby's arrival, Jerome and I participated in Lamaze Birthing Courses, also known as Prenatal Classes. I was very glad that we took the classes because Jerome became an excellent coach. He never liked visiting hospitals, and at first thought, I was certain that he may just pass out in the delivery room. After he saw what a woman had to go through to give birth to a baby, to my surprise, Jerome assisted me in breathing properly and helped me remain calm through the birthing process.

"Push, push!" the nurses said. "The baby is coming. Push!" Out came Patrice. The umbilical cord was cut. Then I really saw her! What a beautiful, healthy baby girl. How precious she was with a head full of black hair. Seven pounds, 12 ounces. It was worth the wait to behold this blessed and wonderful gift from the Father.

The time came for us to take Patrice home. We had her dressed like a little angel. After being placed in her car seat by the nurse, Jerome and I drove her home. My mother had visited our house earlier that morning to make sure it was neat and cozy. Thanks to her, everything was in order upon arriving home, even the nursery. Mother had decorated it so beautifully! Just right for our baby girl!

During the time we were caring for Patrice, we were pretty much homebodies and loved it. I dreaded having to return to work and prayed to find the right caregiver for her while I worked. Just as I asked, we were given the perfect babysitter, Mrs. Head. She happened to be a close friend of my father-in-law's and a member of our family church, Liberty Baptist Church. Glad to take the job as babysitter, she cared for Patrice as if she was her own. Mrs. Head said, "Just bring her

over in her pajamas, and I will feed and bathe her myself."
This was a tremendous help for me because my workday
started at 7:00 am and ended at 3:30 pm.

Pretty much every woman can relate to the struggle of having
to leave their newborn in another's care. I tell you; Mrs. Head
was heaven-sent; she took care of Patrice the first four years
of her life. She later ended her services and relocated to
another state.

Once Mrs. Head relocated, Jerome and I placed Patrice in
Stubb's Daycare. Several of our family members attended
Stubb's Daycare as well, so she was practically in familiar
surroundings. Time went by so rapidly that it was time for
Patrice to advance from Stubb's Daycare to kindergarten.
Toward the end of her kindergarten year, Patrice's teacher
recommended she attend a gifted and talented school
program. She did and continued to excel in her studies.

As life was advancing and adjusting for Patrice, so it was also
for me. When Patrice was three years old, I decided to attend
nursing school at Indiana University. I recall that during our
first group meeting prepared for the nursing students, the
speaker said, "You will be very busy due to our accelerated
curriculum. There will be times when you won't be able to
perform chores, cook, clean, or wash dishes. So be sure to let

your loved ones, spouses, and friends know how strenuous this nursing program will be. You will need their help."

There were many times when I did not get more than a few hours of sleep. Then I would have to get up and rush to school to take the next class. I had night care plans and assignments to complete; then, I had to appear at the hospital to care for my patients. I must say, I would not have made it through if it had not been for Jerome. He was my solid foundation and unshakable help. Jerome went above and beyond the call of duty during that time. He had to comb Patrice's hair many days when I couldn't. Her braids may have been asymmetrical, but he accomplished the task. Jerome made sure to take Patrice to doctor's appointments, assist with school assignments, pickups from daycare, meal preparations, etc.

I am also grateful for how the Lord allowed me to connect with key people to study with, including students who were very disciplined, making A+ grades (those who made the top scores on test and class assignments). The Lord will give you favor.

Psalms 90:17 (ESV)
Let the favor of the Lord our God be upon us, and establish the work of our hands upon us, yes establish the work of our hands!

During the summer of 1990, I graduated from Indiana University Nursing School.

My prayer life budded while I was in college. I would find myself praying to pass tests, praying for increased understanding of class material, etc. I began to notice that many of my prayers were being answered. During that time, I had not actually confessed Jesus Christ as my Lord or asked him to come into my heart and be my savior. I knew that I believed, but I had not surrendered my whole life to him yet. I recall being baptized at an early age. Before confessing, I knew and trusted in the power of prayer, but at this time, I was not disciplined or consistent in prayer, and studying the word of God had not begun for me yet.

So, after eleven years of marriage, who would have thought that the Lord would call Lisa Harris to a "Life" of prayer? It had not always been this way.

Sometime later, I began to pick up the Bible and search it for scripture verses that would line up with whatever I prayed about or prayed for. I believe that prayer changes things.

James 5:16 (NLT)

The earnest prayer of a righteous person has power and produces wonderful results.

Knowing that the prayer of the righteous avails much, which means: Prayers of people in right standing with our heavenly Father brings forth victory.

After graduating from college, my colleagues and I all seemed to go our separate ways. We were all hired to work at different hospitals; we began to meet new people and continued on with our lives. It is incredible how God connects us as individuals at the right time with key people to assist and help propel us into the place of purpose that He desires us to be in.

In choosing the area of nursing focus in the work environment, I initially thought about ICU; however, I reconsidered. Many of my professors and peers felt that it would be more beneficial for me to work on a Medical/Surgical unit first. They felt that getting a solid background knowledge in various types of patient care would be more advantageous for me. Upon meeting with the manager of the Medical/Surgical Telemetry unit, I decided to accept the position. Patient care is truly an excellent form of servanthood. What a joy it is to assist in helping to serve people.

After six years, Jerome and I were expecting our second child. This labor was a lot more challenging than my experience with having Patrice. Jerome was doing all he could to help me through the birthing process, but his sensitivity was not working this time. This little baby decided to position herself right along my lower back. This caused a level of pain that we had not encountered before or anticipated to happen. We made it through. Out came Aerial, just as precious and beautiful as she could be. Once I saw her, the pain was immediately forgotten.

Upon being refreshed and taken to my room, Jerome and I were flooded with balloons and gifts from everywhere. There were so many gifts. It just so happened that our baby was born on the day that my sister Carla had planned the baby shower. I went into labor as we were expecting guests. It was, of course, too late then to cancel, so I gave her the okay to continue with the shower plans. Carla said the shower was beautiful. She brought some gifts to the hospital for the baby and me upon her visit. Some of my friends and co-workers came bearing even more gifts, including those of love and laughter.

I stayed in the hospital for a couple of days. Now it became time to bring our little bundle of joy home. We introduced Aerial to her big sister Patrice. What a delight it was for Patrice.

When the time was nearing for me to return to work, I spoke to Mrs. Head, our former babysitter, who now referred me to consider her niece, Cheryl, as a new babysitter for my newborn. Jerome and I both accepted the consideration. What an excellent help she was to Jerome and me. Cheryl had a set of twin girls that were a few years older than Aerial. So things worked out very well. I knew that I could return to work without worrying or being concerned about my baby girl.

Cheryl happened to be very clean and took excellent care of Aerial. Her children taught her how to do many things, and they played together once the months passed by and Aerial grew older.

My, how time flew. I remember when Aerial was about 18 months old. Jerome was pushing her in her ride-along Princess Carriage Ride-on car while Patrice was about to celebrate a new birthday celebration at Celebration Station, her favorite place of fun. She was pondering over who to invite. Jerome and I helped with the invite list.

What a blessed, happy family we were. Jerome rarely quarreled about anything. Jerome was always mild-tempered, uncomplaining, and willing to go along with most things that I requested. Even when deciding on vacation destinations, we were always in agreement. There were never any monetary issues.

In the earlier years, when money was scarce, we just cut back on certain things, and it worked out. Because of us being one big happy family, it never occurred to me that things could change.

"The Turning Point"

The time had come to surrender all to the Lord. For days, the Lord had been dealing with me in dreams. I was being awakened from sleep, calling on the name of Jesus. At times I would be pleading the blood of Jesus in my dreams.

The last troubling dream caused me to call my sister Brenda. Brenda explained it to me like this, "There is a battle going on. The devil wants to destroy you, and the Lord God wants you to give your life to Him." She said, "There is a church not far from where you live called Deliverance Temple; why don't you visit Sunday?"
I told her that I would attend.

Sunday arrived, and my girls and I attended the community church. As the praise and worship was being led, I could feel myself about to be slain in the spirit, which means go out under the power of God. I had to quickly hold on to the pew to keep from going down to the floor.

I shared my experience with Brenda and told her that I would make a decision regarding giving my life to Christ or not by the following Sunday. This was not difficult for me because I felt that I already had a relationship with the Lord, with whom I often shared many things. My thoughts were to know without a shadow of a doubt that the Father, the Lord, my heavenly Father, the Messiah, was revealing to me that He was ready for me to do His will. I preferred not to have a stranger inform me of this.

CHAPTER 3

Choice Versus Decision

The time was approaching for me to share with Jerome my thoughts on receiving salvation. At that time, total surrender to Christ meant placing God first in my heart, mind, and soul.
I said, "Honey, I am thinking about giving my life to the Lord, getting saved."
He said, "You're already saved. You don't do anything wrong; you have always been a good, loving, and decent person."
Never did I think this conversation would be controversial. The more we talked about it, the louder his voice became.
He said, "You can do what you want, but don't expect me to be a part of it. Most saved people are not living right themselves."
He made it absolutely clear that he did not want me to get saved or receive salvation.

I knew enough about it to acknowledge that Lisa Harris was the only person who had the liberty to make that choice for her life. This kind of decision should only be made between an individual and the Lord. No one can make that decision for you.

Joshua 24:15 (NIV)

Choose this day Whom You will Serve…
As for me and my house, We will Serve the Lord.

Toward the end of the week, the decision was made. During the next Sunday, I went up to the front of the Deliverance Temple Church altar and gave my life to the Lord.

The Elder said, "You can ask the Lord for whatever you want, and He will give it to you."

Well, I asked in prayer for salvation for my husband. Little did I know that there was a price I had to pay for Jerome's salvation. I truly believed that the Lord would save him. However, upon telling Jerome that I had given my life to the Lord, he was not happy at all. He said some angry, hateful, and hurtful words. Before I knew it, I gave it back to him and stormed off. I felt bad about it later and was compelled to repent.

Determined to live for the Lord, I had to be patient and trust the Lord for change, but this was a side of him that had never been seen before, at least not by me. It appeared that when I would go to church, he would hang out with his friends late in the evenings. He would stay out late on bowling nights as well, whereas before, he was always home at night.

Now at this time, Jerome and I had been married eleven peaceful, uneventful years. I would have never imagined our marriage would take such a drastic turn of change.

I said, "The Lord has given me everything that I have, even life itself, and He is calling me to serve Him now. Whatever the cost, I say yes to the Lord."

You see, I was never taught or given instructions on being a saved woman with an unbelieving spouse. We married young, and neither of us were taught about righteousness at that time. So I began to research and study the Bible to understand a wife's responsibilities to her husband as a righteous wife and the responsibilities of an unsaved husband.

I Corinthians 7:14 (KJV)

For the unbelieving husband is sanctified by the wife, and the unbelieving wife is sanctified by the husband: else were your children unclean, but now are they Holy.

I Peter 3:1 (KJV)

Likewise, ye wives, be in subjection to your own husbands; that, if any obey not the word, they also may without the word be won by the conversation of the wives.

So, after reading these scripture verses, I thought that as a woman in right standing with the Lord, I had the ability to help win my husband to Christ. I truly believed that this could be done by the righteous life I lead before him. Let me be clear; my husband grew up as a child attending church, believed that Jesus Christ was the son of God, but was not in right standing with Him as he became an adult. Jerome stopped attending church on a consistent basis, and he was not reading the word of God. He was living his life his way, the way he wanted to live it - without regard to what the heavenly Father purposed for his life. Many believed that Jesus died to save us of our sins and yet are far from Him. They may not have any fellowship with Him and spend no time with Him. Many may not have confessed that Jesus Christ is Lord and asked him to come into their hearts and to be their savior and Lord.

II Corinthians 5:17 (KJV)

Therefore if any man be in Christ, he is a new creature: old things have passed away; behold, all things are become new.

This Bible verse means you no longer want to do the things you used to do that do not line up with the word of God.

I began to realize the difference when I told Jerome that I had decided to and ultimately gave my life to the Lord. He told me not to mention God to him.

Of course, a feeling of hurt tried to take root and emotionalism, but I had to keep my focus on my goal. To live a life before him of righteousness and holiness so that the Father would restore and heal his soul. In doing so, I disciplined myself to read the word of the Lord daily. I began to read several chapters at a time in one sitting. During this time, I recall having a strong desire to read the word of God.

In attending church services, as the message was being taught, I would write it down in my journal and meditate on it later. The church I attended had one-hour prayer meetings on Monday through Thursday from noon until one o'clock. I would attend the prayer meetings on my off days and on days when I was scheduled to work evenings. That was how I became disciplined and learned to pray. I was taught that prayer is how we communicate with the Lord God and one of the many ways He communicates with us.

I would come before the Lord, kneel at His feet, cry out to Him, and He would refresh me. What a powerful weapon we have in Him. We can come before Him in reverence and gratefulness for all he has done for us. Communicate with Him, and He speaks to us exactly what we need to know. He gives us strength for our journey. Nothing can compare to the love and outpouring of His spirit upon us. It is a secret place. He takes away all worry and fear as we kneel before Him in prayer. What a great love that He has for us. Such love that He would lay down His life for us so we would be able to come before Him, ask in prayer for help and trust Him to answer our prayers. Prayer is a direct line of communication with the Father. What an amazing love.

Once I decided to completely follow the Lord and find out about his amazing love for me, I noticed that my spiritual life soared. However, my marriage and family life began to be challenged.

CHAPTER 4

A Husband's Perspective

Many times in life, we may see or view things in a different light. My opinion may not line up with another's opinion, but we are all entitled to our own perspective on things. We all have a choice. Your story may be different from mine. The way one person views and chooses to tell his or hers may not look like the way another expresses their story. They may have the same trials but could see them in total contrast to each other.

Many would ask what could cause a relationship to change abruptly after one commits to the Lord while the other partner remains the same. A relationship is never one-sided; there are always two sides to every love story. In view of this, I, Lisa Harris, interviewed Jerome.

Questions Asked of Spouse

Question #1

When you were a child and old enough to think about what you wanted to be when you became an adult, what did you want to be?

"To be rich and have a big family with lots of children," Jerome responded. He also said he planned to take his children to different places. His family would travel the world. Jerome said, "While growing up, my family didn't have a lot of money to travel much." The family went on trips with their community church in the summer. "We went on picnics and to amusement parks etc. My family never flew on airplanes to various destinations as I grew up as a child. Yet I did have lots of fun doing other things with my siblings. I had a great childhood; I never felt unloved. I had wonderful parents."

Question #2

What did you think of me when you first met me?

"I knew you were a good person. You have a great heart. I felt that you were one of the best people that I had ever met. I really liked you and wanted a chance to be your boyfriend."

Question #3

What offices did you hold at church?

"I sang in the choir and later became an usher in the church."

Question #4

What made you decide to sing in the choir and later become an usher in church?

"Well, my mother made me. She said I had to serve in God's house. My friends in church were ushers, so I decided to be an usher."

Question #5

What was the hardest thing you had to deal with when your wife received salvation?

"Things did change once my wife received the Lord. Where we once did everything together, now she didn't want to watch certain movies if they had too much swearing or cursing in them. We began to do things separately. She would go to church on Sundays with the children, but I did not desire to go. That wasn't my thing, so she went to church several times a week while I went bowling. We did come together during some family times, like vacations and school conferences, but there was a disconnect in our relationship.

"Love is a decision, and as Lisa's mate, I decided and chose to make her my wife. I meant it when I said, "I do" to her before our friends and family. Never did the thought come to my mind to divorce. Divorce was not an option for me."

Question #6

If you could change anything about the time when your wife received salvation, what would it be?

"I would not change anything. I couldn't ask you to be anything other than who you are. Because if I did, I would be asking you to lie. Many people live with their spouses trying to be what their spouse would like them to be instead of being who they really are. This may be for many various reasons, but how could a marriage like that stand?"

Question #7

How do you feel now about me being saved?

"I don't have a problem with you being saved. I've also received salvation. You must be who you are and who the Father purposed you to be. Just as I must be who I am and who the Father purposed me to be. I married Lisa Harris for life. If something ever were to happen to you, I will never marry again. It would be hard to trust anyone else like I trust you. Everything I have in my life I built with you."

Question #8

Do you see or look at me differently now since I've been saved for over 20 years?

"Yes, because the longer a person has been involved in something, the more polished they become. You now know more things about living that type of lifestyle. We've both grown together and learned more concerning this lifestyle. "When we care about people, we accept them for who they are, not for who we want them to be. We all want to be accepted in one way or another. Even when I asked for your hand in marriage, and you said yes, that was an act of acceptance. I accepted the whole you, not part of your life. I was elated, and I've never regretted it. I love Lisa Marie Harris and always will."

CHAPTER FIVE

Victory Versus Defeat

Right thinking is very important. If we think of good things, we will receive good things.

Proverbs 23:7 *(KJV)*
For as he thinketh in his heart so is he:

With positive thoughts, we receive the positive. If we plan to be interviewed for a position and think, 'Oh, I'm not good enough; I don't think they will hire me,' most likely, you will not get the job. We must think about positive things.

John 10:10 *(NIV)*
The thief comes only to steal and kill and destroy;

The thief is known as Satan, the devil, or the evil one. He has many characteristics. One of his main characteristics is that he is a Liar. We have an enemy that speaks things to our minds that are lies.

He would say things to Jerome like, "Lisa doesn't love you anymore; she has found God now." Jerome would then say things like, "God listens to you, Lisa; he doesn't listen to me. I can't do that; I can't walk that believer's walk. I know I can't." All lies! You see, that's what Satan does: interjects wrong thoughts, speaking and rehearsing them over and over again. He can cause our hearts to be filled with unforgiveness, deep hurt, strife, jealousy, blame, etc. If we accept these wrong thoughts, not knowing who is behind them, we allow the devil to destroy homes and cause division in relationships. Satan knows that our Father God loves marriage and has ordained it to be a blessing. That's why the enemy constantly tries to fight against marriage relationships. The truth is, we don't have to accept his lies.

As believers, we have the power in our tongues to cast down imaginations and lies spoken by the evil one.

II Corinthians 10:4, 5 (KJV)

(For the weapons of our warfare are not carnal, but mighty through God to the pulling down of strong holds;)
Casting down imaginations, and every high thing that exalteth itself against the knowledge of God, and bringing into captivity every thought to the obedience of Christ;

John 10:10 (NIV)

But Jesus said, "I have come so that they may have life, and have it to the full."

Whereas the thief takes life, Jesus gives life by His amazing love, forgiveness, and guidance. Jesus gives us the ability to cast down imaginations or mental images that are not real; they are deceptions and lies. Through the Lord God, we have the ability to resist wrong thoughts coming from the enemy by bringing thoughts captive that don't line up with the word of God. When the words spoken by the enemy come, we must resist them by recognizing they are not the voice of the Lord. We can speak and say, "I don't receive those words." Apply the word of God to resist the voice of the devil. Speak forth the opposite of what Satan says by speaking what the word of God says.

During this time, Jerome was not taught how to renew his mind. He had no concept of casting down imaginations and choosing the right thoughts, which caused the enemy to bring anger, jealousy, disappointment, and bitterness into our marriage.

I began to recognize and obtain an understanding that this was not my husband. This is the work of the devil trying to control Jerome by injecting wrong thoughts into his mind. Satan was trying to destroy our marriage by constantly causing negative thoughts and images about me to flood my husband's intellect. The joy and peace we once had in our home were being stolen by Satan.

Somehow something inside me rose up and began to take authority over my marriage and the devil by resisting Satan through prayer, fasting, and the word of God.

II Corinthians 10:4 *(NIV)*

The weapons we fight with are not the weapons of the world. On the contrary, they have divine power to demolish strongholds.

I used the weapons of prayer, some fasting at times, and the word of God. I would wake up early in the morning for years, praying and seeking the Lord on behalf of my husband. I began to pray for my husband's heart, mind, and soul. I prayed that God would heal our marriage and help it to be the marriage that the Lord intended it to be. I prayed that God would help me to be the wife that He intended me to be. These are some of the scriptures I would pray for my husband.

Favorite Scriptures Concerning My Spouse

1.   *Psalms 51:10* (NIV)

      Create in me a pure heart, O God, and renew a steadfast spirit within me.

2.   *Matthew 22:37* (NIV)

      Jesus replied, "Love the Lord your God with all your heart and with all your soul and with all your mind."

3.   *Mark 10:9* (NIV)

      "Therefore what God has joined together, let no one separate."

4.   *I John 4:4* (RSV)

      Little children, you are of God, and have overcome them; for he who is in you is greater than he who is in the world.

5.   *Psalms 1:1* (NIV)

      "Blessed is the one who does not walk in step with the wicked or stand in the way that sinners take, or sit in the company of mockers."

6.   *Psalms 119:2,3 (NIV)*

"Blessed are those who keep his statutes and seek him with all their hearts - they do no wrong but follow his ways."

As I quoted these scriptures and other scriptures, I would place my husband's name in the scripture verse. I declared and decreed that it would be done in Jesus' name. This became a confession of prayer done with consistency for about two years. This form of discipline turned into intercession with no visible change noticed. But I continued to pray daily for him, trusting and thanking the Lord God for my husband's salvation and agreement in our relationship. Sometimes I was at a low place in my faith walk concerning this matter, but the Lord always helped me to continue and maintain my focus on victory and not giving up.

Everyone has challenges they must go through. We cannot give up; our blessing is waiting around the corner for us if we faint not. Let's continue to persevere despite the difficulties placed before us. We cannot give in.

Matthew 24:13 (ESV)

The race is not given to the swift or strong, but he who endures to the end shall be saved.

When two people make the decision to marry one another, there are three great components needed in the marriage. Place the Lord as the head of your relationship, mutual respect, and trust one another. These are very important components of a blessed relationship. The joy of the Lord overflows in couples when they are united. When they are on one accord, having the same vision, and speaking the same things.

Jerome had great plans for our life, but his number one goal was to keep me safe. Once the children came along, he began to make sure that our safety was intact. Jerome would call daily while at work to confirm that we were in the house by a certain time. He would check to ensure that we didn't forget to lock up everything.

In our early years of marriage, we had a little, but what we had, we were happy about it. We never regretted or complained about what we had. We could pay our monthly bills and put food on the table, but there was not much left over. We were in our wealthy place. A place of peace, happiness, joy, and contentment filled our house.

One day I was on my way to the bakery and saw his favorite chocolate iced covered donuts. I purchased some for him. When I gave him the donuts, he had such an expression of gratitude on his face; you would have thought I had bought him a new pair of shoes. It didn't take much to please him. We were always doing things or buying things to please one another. We could hardly wait to get home from work to talk to each other about our day. On my days off, I would try to have his dinner prepared when he arrived home. He would be happy that I cooked him something special. Jerome wasn't difficult to please. He never got upset if I didn't cook a meal on certain days. He was content with almost everything that I did. He was what we called an easy-going man, relaxed and understanding. He would do the laundry, take care of yard work, and car maintenance. I took care of the indoor work of cleaning and keeping things in order. Everything just fitted together nicely. What marital bliss. He would call me pretty head or pretty face. I would call him Honey or Rome. We just enjoyed our special times and made our house a home.

Later in life, Jerome and I were more prosperous. I had received my degree as a registered nurse, and Jerome worked as a tile setter in Illinois. Patrice, our firstborn, was placed in Stubb's Daycare during that time. Jerome or I would get off work and pick up Patrice, or she would be dropped off at home. Next, we would pick up Aerial, our youngest daughter, from her babysitter's home. Jerome and I would usually get home from work around the same time. I would prepare dinner; we would eat, play with the children and prepare for the next workday.

I thought, 'I want this happy, trusting, fulfilling family life back.' I decided that, whatever I had to do to get our happy home back, I must give it a try.

Jerome would say, "I didn't choose this righteous way of life; you did. I'm not going to change."

I was not concerned about the words Jerome spoke to me about not changing. I trusted God and continued to believe. I thanked the Lord for saving my husband, even though he was not saved at the time.

There was a time that I confessed portions of the scriptures in **Psalms 119 (KJV)** over my husband's life.

For example, verse 7 says:

I will praise thee with uprightness of heart, when I shall have learned thy righteous judgments.

I was focused, determined, and believed with everything in me that our heavenly Father would save Jerome's soul and place within him the desire to seek Him with his whole heart. I believed that then, Jerome and I would be on one accord in total agreement and unity, as a married couple should be.

I began to sense that a turnaround in our marriage was near. Jerome started to ask me upon coming home from church,

"How was church service today?" That was my opportunity to share a little about the message our Pastor spoke on. At times, Jerome would go to church with me upon my asking him to. I would feel excited and in great anticipation, thinking this might be when he says yes completely to the Lord, but later realized that this was not the day.

At times it felt like riding a Ferris wheel, going around and around, up and down. I thought, 'When will it be over?' Yet our God is a keeper. He will sustain and keep your focus when your mind remains on him. Nobody but the Lord can keep you in perfect peace and give you the ability to continue to stay the course. He allows you to keep trusting and believing that joy is coming in the morning for your marriage.

CHAPTER SIX

For Better or For Worse

One of Jerome and my gravest mistakes we made before marriage was not communicating with one another about our religious values and beliefs. This was an area that Jerome and I happened not to discuss before marriage. We didn't know then what we know now. Obstacles could have been avoided if we had sought premarital counseling. During the time we were considering marriage, we didn't even know that premarital counseling even existed. However, there are also some things that cannot be foreseen. But no matter what, we know that there is always someone we can turn to. His name is Jesus.

This is the time when I secretly began to intercede* for my spouse and marriage with increased intensity. While praying on his behalf, I began to see a change take place in my husband as intercession continued to be made. I began to do some things differently. For example, he would be downstairs watching television, and instead of remaining upstairs doing my own thing, I started joining him. I would maybe make some popcorn and watch a movie with him. I started to spend some quality time with him consistently, which helped us get reconnected with one another.

There were times when he allowed me to read the Bible to him. I would ask what the scriptures meant to him after reading them. He would share his interpretation of the Bible, and I would always be amazed at his analysis. It made me realize how great his understanding was of what I read. Sometimes, I would intercede for hours on certain days, but less on others. Many times Jerome would ask me if I had been praying for him.

*DEFINITION: INTERCEDE
1. Intervening on someone's behalf through prayer
2. Petition in favor of another, without them knowing it.
3. Praying to the deity on behalf of oneself or others. [5]

Little by little, Jerome's spiritual eyes were being opened. He would bring friends by the house when they were experiencing challenges and ask me to pray for them. Sometimes he would give me the name of someone he knew and ask me to pray for them. Later Jerome would reveal to me how his friends' lives had changed after they had received prayer. The ability to talk to the Father on behalf of another without their knowing is a powerful act. It will fill your heart with joy and a sense of accomplishment. Doors of opportunity open when intercession is going on. Miracles happen in the spirit, causing manifestation on the earth.

We must recognize that spiritual battles are authentic. They are serious because we are in conflict with an enemy who can't be seen but happens to be very real. Our truth is that our Lord Jesus Christ, who is the King of Kings and Lord of Lords and is to become the Almighty, shows up when we need him or call upon him for assistance. God has given us the power to overcome the enemy. He has given us the ability, the authority, and power, once we receive him, to overcome the enemy through prayer, fasting, faith, and perseverance. We have spiritual weapons to defeat the enemy.

Spiritual Weapons to Defeat the Enemy

1. Prayer and intercession
2. The Word of God
3. Peace of God (knowing that you have the victory)
4. Righteousness
5. Faith (belief)
6. Praise and worship

It is essential to know the root causes of your spouse not surrendering his/her will to God the Father. It is known that fear is one of Satan's greater mechanisms he uses against people because he knows that fear diminishes faith.

Hebrews 11:6 (NIV)

And without faith it is impossible to please God, because anyone who comes to him must believe that he exists and that he rewards those who earnestly seek him.

We must believe that whatever we ask the Father for, He will give it to us. We must ask without wavering. The thing that we are trusting and believing for, we must stand on and never give up on it, even if we don't see it. Until it comes to pass, thank God for it.

Prayer: Deliverance from Fear

Father, You have not given (name of spouse) a spirit of fear, but a spirit of power, and of love, and of a sound mind. You are (spouse's name) deliverer from all fear. Thank you for setting (spouse's name) free from the fear of rejection and ridicule. (Spouse's name) will not be intimidated by others because You, Father, God are his/her helper. {My spouse will not fear or dread or be terrified.} With all encounters in this life, you, (spouse's name), are an overcomer by the blood of Jesus and by the word of your testimony.
In the precious name of Jesus, amen.[1]

After enduring the same trials for a substantial period of time, I find that anger, judgment, impatience, and holding grudges can begin to take root in our lives without us knowing that we are experiencing these characteristics. Then we wonder why these negative actions are occurring. With every action, there is a response. Maybe if we had known to ask the Lord to heal us from these wrong characteristics, we could have confessed them and asked the Lord to remove them from us. We could have been healed from them long ago.

When the root of bitterness tries to overtake us, it is possible that we may be harboring deep hurt or unforgiveness. We could be dwelling on thoughts of how unfairly we have been treated - concentrating, meditating, and focusing on the injustice so much that unforgiveness takes root in us. These thoughts can cause a person or people to sink into the trap of bitterness and revenge.

Know that there is healing available. Turn to Jesus, the one and only healer of our soul. He will restore you and make you or your spouse whole. He is waiting on us. Recognize the problem and act on His plan for your life. He will restore joy, peace, and comfort in your home. Ask Jesus to come into your marriage and break the chains of bitterness off of your family and home.

Prayer: To Overcome Bitterness

Father, you have esteemed marriage as something beautiful. You know what we have been through.
Lord, help us to let go of bitterness (anger, discontentment, rage, unforgiveness, strife).
You are the one who binds up and heals the brokenhearted. I receive your anointing, which destroys yokes of bondage and heals the broken. I receive emotional healing by faith, and I thank you for giving me the ability to be strong and take courage until the process is complete.
In the name of Jesus, I choose to forgive those who have wronged me. I plan to live a life of forgiveness because You have forgiven me.

DEFINITION: ENCOURAGEMENT

To fill with courage or strength of purpose, especially in preparation for a hard task or while going through a hard task.[2]

After going through some difficult times, we must take courage. Endure trials as a good soldier. Be joyous and persevere in all things. Say positive things about yourself. Speak words like, "Be anxious for nothing; know that you will reap if you do not faint or give up. Joy is coming soon. No matter what it looks like. Believe that all things work together for good for those who love the Lord. Encourage yourself in the Lord. Say that *I can do all things through Christ who gives me strength.*[1] I'm more than a conqueror; I am an overcomer. *I am the head and not the tail, above and not beneath.*[2] I am the righteousness in Christ Jesus. *Who can separate me from the love of Christ?*[3] Nothing can. I am beautiful and wonderfully made. *Greater is he that is in me than he that is in the world.*[4] I am blessed."

[1]Philippians 4:13 (NIV), [2]Deuteronomy 28:13 (KJV), [3]Romans 8:35 (KJV), [4]1 John 4;4 (KJV)

I had to speak these things with authority, and the discouragement, loneliness, depression, and sadness left me as I confessed these words about my life. I began to speak about what I wanted to see, not what I saw. I confessed the two shall be as one:

Jerome and Lisa walk in complete agreement. Jerome loves his wife as Christ loves the church. Jerome honors and respects his wife and places her above all others except the Lord. The Lord has restored the love of Jerome and Lisa's youth.

Lisa honors and respects her husband. Lisa ministers to Jerome and views him as the King in their home. Lisa is a helper to her husband and looks up to him. Lisa spends quality time with Jerome, her husband. Lisa is learning to listen to her husband because my heavenly Father speaks through him.

Father, because marriage is a covenant between you, my mate Jerome, and me (Lisa), we ask that you will help us to lift one another up in prayer.

Marriage Prayer

Father God, help us to remember the time when we first met and fell in love. To remember the strong love that grew between us. Help us love in an unselfish way, placing one another's needs above our own, so that nothing can divide us or come between us. May our words be kind, and our thoughts be gracious. May we remain humble of heart to ask for forgiveness, and wise in spirit to give to one another freely. In Jesus' name, we pray, amen.

I Corinthians 13:4-8 (NIV)

Love is patient, love is kind. It does not envy, it does not boast, it is not proud.
It does not dishonor others, it is not self-seeking, it is not easily angered, it keeps no record of wrongs.
Love does not delight in evil but rejoices with the truth.
It always protects, always trusts, always hopes, always perseveres.
Love Never Fails.

There comes a time in our prayer life when we enter a season of rest. You've been praying, fasting, and interceding, but now is your time of rest. I am not talking about a physical rest involving napping and not being active. I am talking about spiritual rest from worrying, stress, and unbelief - entering a place of knowing that it is already done. Your miracle is on the way. How do you know this? You will know this when you are at peace in your waiting. During this time, rest means you have reached an increase in your level of faith.

Hebrew 11:1 (KJV)
Now faith is the substance of things hoped for, the evidence of things not seen.

This is the time when you thank the Lord for manifesting or bringing forth what you have been praying for, even though you have not seen it come to pass. For example, you have been praying for a new car, but you don't have it yet. Say, "Thank you, Lord, for giving me my new car."

Matthew 21:22 (NIV)

If you believe, you will receive whatever you ask for in prayer.

I remember it was an early Sunday morning, and I said to Jerome, "Would you like to give your life to the Lord?"
He said, "Let me think about it. I'll let you know in a week or two."
I said, "Alright, you know that at our church there is a card that says, 'Become a member,' and all you have to do is fill it out."
He said, "Okay."

A week passed by, then another, when the Holy Spirit whispered and said, "Ask Jerome if he would like to join the church."
I hesitated for a few minutes, then located Jerome and said, card in hand, "Would you like to join our church?"
Running behind in his schedule, he replied, "I am in a hurry. You fill it out for me. I am running late for work."

"Okay," I simply replied, so excited that I jumped up and down the moment he left for work, thinking to myself, 'Yes! It is done.'

I can't express how grateful to the Lord I felt. I knew that now we were on one accord. I thought now nothing we ask for, according to the will of God in prayer, shall we be denied. I also knew that the Heavenly Father would continue to work on Jerome and me and guide us into the place that He has for us to be. I began to sense a shift in our home and relationship. No longer were we married, living separate lives, but we grew closer to one another and began considering each other.

When I entered into the rest of God, I no longer had to fear or be discouraged. We had now entered the place of trust - trusting and believing that it's already done.

Proverbs 3:5 (NIV)

Trust in the Lord with all your heart and lean not on your own understanding, in all your ways submit to Him, and He will make our paths straight.

Your peace, Lord, that calms the boisterous, unruly, raging waters of the sea, let it comfort me and my family.

Psalms 23 (NIV)

The Lord is my shepherd, I lack nothing. He makes me lie down in green pastures, he leads me beside quiet waters, he refreshes my soul. He guides me along the right paths for his name's sake.

Peace (Poem)

I close my eyes and I breathe You in,
Your presence, Your spirit, Your peace
Peace like a river overtakes me,
All the cares of the world fall away
I am weightless, I am content,
Content to be in this moment with You,
I breathe you in and there is peace,
Your peace surpasses all understanding
By: Patrice N. Harris

CHAPTER SEVEN

A Marriage Restored

On the next Sunday, Jerome and I went to church together. During the closing of our church service, our Pastor, right before the altar call, asked everyone to close their eyes and to repeat after him. He said, "Father, forgive me of my sins. I believe that you are the son of God. I ask you to come into my heart and be my savior and be my Lord."

Jerome and many others confessed with their mouths the sinner's prayer and gave their lives to the Lord.

After confessing with their mouths Jesus Christ and believing in their hearts that Jesus is the son of God, they became children of the kingdom of God.

It was just that simple. This is the man who once told me not to mention the Lord to him. The heavenly Father has changed his heart.

Although salvation is a great accomplishment, it should never be taken for granted. Prayer is always in order, for we go from glory to glory, platform to platform, victory to victory, story to story, and blessing to blessing.

I John 4:4 (NKJV)

Because greater is he that is in you, than he that is in the world.

There are always greater levels available for us who are in Christ to achieve. Although things are already much brighter in my family and home, I believe that my husband and I will come to have a deeper relationship with the Lord. Most people in society often want a quick fix, myself included; we want to snap our fingers and say, "Voila! It is done." However, there is more to it than peace and tranquility in my home of unity and salvation for my spouse. There is another level. We must ask ourselves, just as I had to, what's next? Am I on fire for God, is my spouse on fire for Him? What will He have for us to accomplish next? Should we stop here and be content, or should we come closer and listen to hear what the Lord has for my spouse and me to accomplish next?

The answer is yes; it is time to come closer and go deeper in the word of the Lord while praying for intimacy with the Father. We must spend more time in His presence. We must first have the desire to come close. If you see that you are ready to get closer and your spouse is not, you should pray for him or intercede for him in the secret place. It is possible that you may be in a different place or on another level than your spouse. Continue to stay in love with him and pray for him until the Father gives you the victory over it. Sometimes there are hindrances to your prayers, but don't give up. Stay in faith, not wavering. Some things take time. Some things occur by prayer only.

Mark 9:29 (NIV)
He replied, "This kind can come out only by prayer."

Early Morning Prayer

Father, I pray that Jerome and I make room for the Lord today. Help us to be focused on your plans. Allow us to abide in your presence at work, in our homes, and wherever we go today. Show Jerome and me how to put you first in our lives. For we know that if we seek you first today that everywhere we go, you will be present to help us with every need. Surround us with your love, and keep us safe. Today is the day that you have made; we will rejoice and be glad in it. Draw us closer to you today and help others be healed by words of enlightenment that flow through our mouths.
In Jesus' name, we pray, amen.

Afternoon Prayer

Father, help Jerome and I have a strong hunger for God. That we will chase after you. Reveal your hidden treasures to us so that we will be a blessing to others.

Evening Prayer

Oh that you would bless Jerome and I indeed, cause your face to shine upon us, be gracious to us. We need to be a light in the world. Help us to draw your people back toward you. Open up their hearts to say yes again to your will. Help us to adore you, Lord, most high. Let our words be filled with passion as we praise and honor you.

Even as we stay in faith for our spouses, we must be patient, knowing that the Lord will perfect what concerns us. He always has and always will.

DEFINITION: PATIENCE

The power or capacity to endure without complaint something difficult or disagreeable.

Source: The Merriam-Webster Thesaurus. Page 437

How many of us in this world feel that we have the ability to accept or tolerate delay? Dealing with trouble, disappointment, shame, and suffering without getting upset or downright angry takes a disciplined type of person. Most of us believe that we can handle it until we are faced with something tragic or unsettling. That's when we find out the level of patience we really have. I must say, as a new Christian, after hearing so much from attending Sunday services and bible studies and reading God's Holy Word, you feel like you can accomplish anything. But after growing in my Christian walk, I've found that patience has to be worked through us. For example, like a building being built, there are different stages of the building process to get to completion. Like a baby trying to walk, he or she has to build up the confidence to believe that they can walk and not fall and hurt themselves.

In my faith walk, I started with the belief that I could pray and confess for my husband's salvation, expecting it would happen immediately. When it didn't happen as I thought it would, I had to build up the courage to continue on in faith, standing on the word of God in the process. Not knowing initially that this faith-patience walk would take many years before its manifestation would come.

God wants to produce patience in us to show us how to trust in Him. And without faith, it is impossible to please Him, for he who comes to Him must believe that He is. He is the rewarder of those who diligently seek Him with a sincere heart.

Most times, the Father of all living allows us to triumph over difficult circumstances. Patience may involve our persevering in the face of delay. Having the ability to be tolerant of, instead of responding in anger, vengeance, or disrespect when under persecution, dealing with long-term difficulties, problems, or difficult people. For example, one day, I happened to be working the three to eleven shift and was about to receive a surgical admission. Once she arrived, I began to assist her, trying to make sure that she was comfortably placed in bed, taking vitals, etc. She began to get very loud once she realized that she could not have another dose of medication due to her just receiving a dose in recovery. She was swearing and getting out of control.

I said with a soft, calm voice, "How can I help you? Let me get you settled. I am sorry that you're in so much pain. I will page your doctor to let him know what your pain scale number is and that you're not feeling much pain relief."

I remembered the scripture in Proverbs 15:1 saying, *"a soft answer turns away wrath."* The young lady calmed down almost instantly when she heard the soft, soothing sound of my voice.

DEFINITION: HOPE

Expect, which is the same as hope. To anticipate in the mind.
Synonyms: await, count (on or upon), hope, look; [4]

Most people have something in their hearts or in their minds to accomplish. For one, it may be to graduate from high school, attend college, or go to a business college and complete the program quicker to get a great job faster. Some may want to get married and or have children. How about desiring to own your own business? Whatever it may be, we must do something to obtain it. Hope alone won't cause us to achieve it. We must work toward it. For me, it was a matter of wondering, after receiving my desire, what comes next? I realized that there was another level to my hopes. After my husband received salvation, the next level would be relationship and intimacy with the Father. Through continuing in intercession for my spouse, I began to witness him worshipping the Father in song and the lifting up of his hands to dance and praise God. So when I think of what the Lord has done for Jerome, all I can say is gratefulness.

I am grateful for what God has done already in my husband and my life. When I think back on how far the Lord has brought us, I get excited about what He will do next. I realized that while praying for Jerome, God was actually working on me. During my times of frustration and moments when I was overwhelmed with thoughts to throw in the towel or give up, the Holy Spirit was my help. He allowed me to resist those wrong thoughts from the enemy, the devil.

When discouragement came, the Lord lifted me above my problems. Praise is a weapon. I praised Him in the midst of my trials. God is my help. After you've done all you can stand, don't give up, God will see you through. He did it for me. He will do it for you. Trust Him!

A blessing is not a blessing if you get it before its time. Our heavenly Father knows that if we hope for something and obtain it too soon, we could lose it. Our hearts can change when we receive things that we have not worked or prepared fully for. There is a process we must go through, and once we go through it in its entirety, we will be ready to handle the blessings God has for us.

CHAPTER EIGHT

Happiness

A state of being or pleasurable satisfaction; that's what happiness is. Looking back, there was a time when everything was well with my life. The first eleven years of marriage were wonderful. Towards the end of those eleven years, Jerome and I were increasing in financial stability. Our children were healthy and happy. Jerome and I were happy together. This was before surrendering my all to the Lord.

Even though I was content with my marriage and family at that time, I still felt like something was missing. There was an emptiness that was unshakable - a void that could not be denied. I recall not being able to understand why I felt that way at the time. However, after saying yes to the Lord completely, a joy that overflowed within me surfaced. After twenty-eight years of salvation, I must say, I've never lost that joy inside. Even though trials and tribulations come, as I confess the word of God over them, victory is mine! I quote scriptures such as:

Nehemiah 8:10
The joy of the Lord is my strength.
Psalm 144:15
Happy are the people whose God is the Lord!

Applying the word of God to whatever situation you're going through will bring change. I noticed that as I confessed what His word says, I would, many times, immediately see those things come to pass. The word of God has the power to heal.

Everyone wants to be happy. I am so glad that the Lord rekindled my husband and my relationship. We are happy and work together. Jerome allows me to fulfill my purpose, and I minister to him as God is still working on us both. I feel people are happiest when they are walking the path that God has ordained for them to walk. Now I am truly able to say that the Lord has restored love, joy, and happiness into our lives that once was not there.

I find that I am most happy when I reach out to show kindness and when I help others in need to smile. Happiness to me is the ability to be able to watch the sun rise and set. Peace is my happiness. Playing with my granddaughter and watching my grandchildren grow up makes me happy. My happiness is spending time with my children, laughing, and joking around. In having family gatherings, happiness is to be given away, and in return, it comes back to you.

Happiness is a choice. When the cares of life try to weigh me down, I can choose to be happy. I don't have to accept discouragement, anger, or pain. I can call those things that are not as though they were by confessing what I want to see and applying the word of God to it. Trouble doesn't last forever. I know that I must resist negativity and embrace positivity.

I become happy when I have accomplished something great. Achievement brings joy when you feel like the accomplishment isn't less than you expected. Fulfillment of personal goals and desires can make one happy. To dream and believe in something for so long and finally, it comes true can cause a person to be overwhelmed with happiness and joy.

What is happiness in our world today? What helps us smile on those dreary days? We look inside ourselves when things are blue, but if we trust in Him (the Lord) and give our problems to Him, He will make us brand new.

Family Priorities

A. IN THE PRESENCE OF THE LORD

When thinking of the number one focus concerning happiness, I think of our Lord and Savior, Jesus Christ. When I wake up early in the morning, my first thoughts of the day are about Him. Spending time with the Lord, I first thank him for watching over me all night long. I ask the Lord to lead my family and me throughout the day. I have always been taught to put God first, and because I do, he watches over my family and keeps us safe. God is my provider, my way maker, my peace, and joy. Without Him, there is no peace and joy because He is the giver of all things that are good.

These are not things that I am obligated to do. We have a relationship, and I enjoy doing these things for the Lord. Many times I will worship before Him or play a song of praise, then worship by singing and dancing before Him. As I begin to honor Him in the dance, a feeling of joy fills my heart.

Psalms 100:4
Enter into His gates with thanksgiving and into His court with praise, for God inhabits the praises of His people.

This is the most powerful way to get into the presence of God. Anger, fear, and doubt dissipate when we sing and dance before the Lord. A freedom is released that is almost unexplainable. All of my world is great, and nothing can change it. Joy, unspeakable joy, fills our hearts in the presence of the Lord. Chains break off of people during praise and worship. Chains represent slavery, oppression, and great pain. All negativity and stress dissipate in the presence of the Lord. Great deliverance takes place in His presence.

In the Presence of Royalty (Poem)

Oh sovereign King, how wonderful you are, the one who reigns forever
You are omnipotent and all-powerful, You are holy,
In Your presence, I won't fear for thou art with me,
I bow down in your presence, for I am overwhelmed by your sovereignty
The one who reigns forever,
You are faithful, and you are true.
You are the King who sits on the throne and between the cherubims, high and lifted up.
In Your presence, the angels shout holy, holy.
Demons tremble at Your name. Oh sovereign Father, I'm in awe of You.
By: Patrice N. Harris

B. SPOUSE IN LOVE

A major part of my happiness began when Jerome found me. He knocked at my door. I was just seventeen when this tall, dark, and handsome young man was introduced to me. He wore these shorts that were cut off just above the knees. He had on a white short-sleeve shirt and Nike gym shoes on, not to mention that he had a strawberry-flavored Dairy Queen shake in his hand.

During the dating period, Jerome was so protective of me. He was always a gentleman when we would go to various places, and he would always hold my hand. Even crossing the streets, he would hold my hand and ensure I was safe. As my heavenly Father watched out for me, Jerome also made sure of my protection. Once I became his wife, he never stopped protecting me and providing me with safety.

After the birth of our children, as the years passed by, I experienced great joy and happiness as I realized what a great daddy my husband has been. This continues to be true to this day. Our children graciously honor, respect, and look up to their dad. He would give his last to make sure that his family doesn't want or need anything, even as our Heavenly Father is a great Daddy to me.

I think of how, throughout our courtship, Jerome was very generous. He took me to some of the finest restaurants to dine. Never did he have a problem concerning the cost; he paid for everything. Once I became his wife, he continued to provide for me and our children. Even to this day, we have never had a problem with money. He never squandered our money, and he made sure that all the bills were paid. Just as our Heavenly Father is a wonderful and excellent provider, so is Jerome. So, all in all, our spouses should resemble God, our Heavenly Father.

Words cannot express the unshakeable love Jerome and I have for each other.
Jerome said, "It was love at first sight" when he met me.
I would always reply, "I don't believe that; how can you fall in love at first sight?"
It did not happen that way for me. However, Jerome was so sweet and kind to me; he swept me off my feet. He builds me up and helps to restore me when I need it. My destiny is tied to him.
Jerome said, "Without Lisa, there is no Jerome."
He always says that I am under his protection. He says he is always looking out for me. If he goes to a store without me, he tries to find things that I would enjoy, just as I do the same for him. He is always bringing me gifts. We have become inseparable, but there was a time when we were not. Jerome

went from not wanting me to mention anything about the Lord to my reading the Bible to him often. He prays for me before I go to work and covers me in prayer daily. We now have a family bible study weekly.

So, men and women, don't give up on your spouses. It may just be that the Father might want to use you to help turn them around for His Glory. He can bring happiness to your marriage like you have not experienced before.

C. CHILDREN ADORED

Happiness for me is, mothering my children. They are so precious to me. Each of them has their own different attributes. I love them both.
Growing up, Patrice loved to sing in the mass choir at school. She also enjoyed singing with the choir during community events. Aerial enjoyed playing the violin at school and with her peers during community events. As an adult, Patrice enjoys painting, drawing, writing poetry, the arts, etc. Aerial enjoys having fun, socializing, and spending quality time with her husband and children. They both enjoy traveling. I enjoy spending quality time with them both.

It amazes me how the Lord helped Jerome and me raise such intelligent, smart, professional women who are walking in their purpose. They are humble, uplifting, and a joy to be around. I'm so thankful for the level of integrity they are blessed to walk in. I'm not just writing these things about them because they are my children, but God knows it is the truth. My happiness involves my children.

Children are gifts from God. The Bible says to train your children. My husband and I used the word of God to assist in raising our children. They were taught how to follow Christ. They saw their dad and mother going to church. Our children attended church on a regular weekly schedule, but we also allowed them to have fun with their peers. They went to supervised parties, children's fun houses and played outside with children in the neighborhood. They went bike riding and bowled in a children's bowling league etc.

Proverbs 22:6 (KJV)
Train up a child in the way he should go; when he is old, he will not depart from it.

Psalms 127:3 (KJV)
Lo, children are an heritage of the Lord; and the fruit of the womb is His reward.

This means children are one of our greatest assets or blessings that come from the Lord. They have the ability to shape the future. God values them so highly.

D. GRAND PLEASURE

Oh, what treasures of happiness our grandchildren give! Blessings from above, wrapped in love. The relationship we have with our grandchildren is so very special. We provide unconditional love to our grandchildren. How wonderful it is to watch them grow up and mature into respectable individuals. It is a valuable time to share things with them that will help them along in their lives. We enjoy listening to what they have to say. They fill our home with laughter every time they stay. I adore singing lullabies and teaching them to pray.

As a grandmother, I love holding my grandchildren. I love putting them down to sleep. I love purchasing frilly things for my granddaughter to wear. Jerome and I cherish the precious times we have with them. Whether we're choosing stories, sharing a book, going to the park, or they're watching us cook and work on projects, these times we will remember - they'll never be overlooked.

Bonding with family is one of the greatest gifts the Father can give. So we thank you, Father, for restoring our family unit. Thank you for your everlasting love. Through your words, you have taught us the importance of family. Jerome and I pray that you will continually help us to always put you first. Father, help us always to show one another love and kindness. As a family, may we treat each other with compassion. Let your peace and happiness forever reside in our homes.

I sometimes think about what could have happened if I had given up on my husband and our marriage. I do know that I would not be complete without him. My family would not have been whole if one of the most important parts had been removed or taken out of it. For example, can an eagle fly without one wing? My children could have gone through life missing the close, special relationship that they have with their dad.

CHAPTER NINE

A Marriage on One Accord

Love is most important in a marriage relationship. A marriage on one accord has priorities and levels of authority. These levels start with the love of God, the love of a spouse, the love of our children, working to provide for the family, the love for local church family and friends.

I: The Love of God

Jerome and I place our Father God first in our relationship now. We acknowledge Him in all we do. We pray for one another in the morning, trusting the Father to protect us as we maneuver throughout the day. Jerome and I also have our own personal relationship with God. We read the word of God together then we expound on what we have read. Also, throughout the day, we put into practice what we have read.

II: The Love of a Spouse

Ephesians 5:22-25 (NIV)

Wives, submit yourselves to your own husbands as you do to the Lord. For the husband is the head of the wife as Christ is the head of the church, his body, of which he is the savior. Now as the church submits to Christ, so also wives should submit to their husbands in everything. Husbands love your

*wives, just as Christ loved the church and gave himself up for
her.*

After God, we both made the decision to place no one higher
than each other in our marriage. Of course, we love our
children, family, and friends, but we know that after God the
Father, our next priority is each other. Our fellowship with
each other is important. We must stay connected by spending
quality time with one another. Interacting with each other
keeps us united and bonded together.

Mark 10:9 (NKJV)

Therefore what God has joined together, let not man separate.

Marriage is a Holy act, done before God and witnessed by
man. A man and woman make a vow or pledge to one
another. Confessing their love for one another and vowing to
love, honor, and cherish each other. We as mates should not
allow anything to separate us. We are to be inseparable,
encourageable, and sincere in the bond of Holy matrimony.
We are to work together and let nothing separate us from the
love of God and our love for each other. The two, husband
and wife, shall be one flesh, working things or situations out
together, trusting in one another, protecting one another.
Vows are important, so don't give up on your marriage to one
another. Trust God to restore your marriage as he restored

ours. Nothing is too hard for God. If the husband or wife is pleased to dwell with their spouse, then your marriage is worth saving.

Allow the Lord time to work on your marriage relationship. Pour out your heart to Him. Ask God to fix whatever the problems are. Begin to wait patiently while praying, believing, and thanking God for working the problems and concerns out. Just as He did it for Jerome and me, he will do it for you.

Matthew 7:7 (NKJV)
Ask, and it shall be given you; seek, and you will find; knock, and it will be opened to you.

Our God is not a respecter of persons. What He does for one, he will do for another. God will provide every person the opportunity to receive blessings when we live in an honest, correct manner before Him. It is His good pleasure to help us. All we have to do is ask.

Psalms 34:19 (KJV)
Many are the afflictions of the righteous: but the Lord delivereth him out of them all.

So yes, we do have challenges in this life. One individual may go through this, another that, but the Lord always delivers or brings us out of every challenging situation. All we have to do is ask Him and believe that he can and will fix it. Believe me; He will. He is waiting on us to give it to Him and to trust Him. The God of all creation is the deliverer. He rescues and sets free. He frees us from disappointment, despair, trials, and hardship. We can come to Him. He will restore joy where there is pain. He brings peace when there is chaos. He bears our burdens. He is the Lord of the breakthrough.

No matter how bad the situation might look or how massive the problem is, there is nothing too hard for our God. Even in the most extreme cases, I am a living witness. God will deliver and bring every high place low.

III. The Love of Our Children

As parents, we have the responsibility of raising our children in a way that is pleasing to God the Father. We must show them our love, which enables them to show love towards others. Parents, caregivers, foster parents, etc., have an obligation to discipline their children in the correct way. Discipline is an act of love. We are obligated to teach our children what is right and wrong. Children must be taught to obey their parents, adults, teachers, and other important role models in the community. They should know that there are consequences of positive and negative behavior. Parents also have a responsibility to teach their children who the Father God is.

Proverbs 22:6

Train up a child in the way he should go; even when he is old
he will not depart from it.

Reading the Holy Bible to your child, taking them to church,
and praying with them are excellent ways to introduce children
to Father God.

IV. Working Brings an Income Stability

Having a steady job is important. It is a means for providing
income into the home to pay the house note or rent, car
payment, school tuition, gas bills, etc. There are other benefits
to working a steady job. It not only ensures that you will obtain
a regular paycheck, but it also provides you with a means of
learning new skills and meeting new people. Although working
is important, balance and family time are just as important.

V. Christians/Local Church

Our brothers and sisters in Christ, our spiritual family, are
important. If they have a concern or problems, we should be
helpful and sensitive to their needs. It is a blessing to help one
another. As members of the body of Christ, we are to serve in
the ministry and family of God. We are to follow the proper
protocol.

VI. Biological family and friends and others

Indeed, we adore our biological family, friends, and associates; however, we must not allow them to interfere negatively in our marriage. Marriage is Holy and must be respected, remembering that husbands and wives are required to respect and honor each other in the ways that God ordains.

Keep in mind that priority in a marriage and keeping our vows cuts down much confusion, disagreements, and disappointments. It brings in Godly order. We should neither put the children before God in our marriage nor place work before our spouse because we would definitely be out of order. Being out of order in marriage can create an opening for the devil to enter into our relationships and cause disparaging situations. When we follow the order of priorities in our marriage, as mentioned earlier, it can defend us against attacks from the devil. For example, our obedience stands like a steel wall or barrier in place preventing Satan from entering into our marital relationships.

For years, we went through the motions of heading to work, greeting one another when we got home from work, eating dinner, spending time with our children, and preparing for the next day. While my husband was downstairs watching television all evening, I was doing my own thing upstairs.

Living separate lives, divided. It was not a place of pleasure at all, especially when you know in your heart that marriage is supposed to be so much better than this. Remembering that we had experienced such betterment in the past only brought hurt, disappointment, and shame. I was going to church and other events week after week, and people were asking where my husband was. I have wondered how I could have endured this for so many years. How could my husband have suffered through this as well? It had to have been just as difficult for him as it was for me. Believe me, I didn't see it this way while going through it. I was only focused on my own pain. Only through the strength of God Almighty could we have endured it. We had to learn to forgive each other.

CHAPTER TEN

Forgive

DEFINITION: to cease to feel resentment against (an offender): PARDON // forgive one's enemies [3]

The word of God says:

Matthew 6:14 (NIV)
For if you forgive other people when they sin against you, your heavenly Father will also forgive you.

Mark 11:24 (NKJV)
Father God, Jesus your son said, whatever things you ask for when you pray, believe that you receive them and you will have them.

Prayer to Receive Forgiveness
Father God, I come humbly before you today to ask you to forgive me of all my sins. Forgive me for things that I should have done and didn't do in my home and marriage. Forgive me for words that I did not speak when I should have spoken them, and for words I spoke that I should not have spoken to my spouse. I ask you to forgive me for every wrong thought that was not from you, Lord. Restore my home and marriage.

Help my spouse and me to return to the loving relationship we once knew. Rekindle the flames of Holy matrimony again in our lives. These things I ask in Jesus' name.

I believe every word mentioned in this prayer, and if there is any doubt in my heart, I ask that you remove it. Thank you, Lord, for forgiving me. Your generosity is overwhelming. I am so grateful for your love.

Once you have forgiven one another, then the Father will begin to forgive you and restore your marriage and family.

Reconnect With your Partner

Find ways to reconnect with one another again. Remember and think of things that you both did when you were dating one another. Begin to date again. Plan and schedule one on one time with each other. Times of intimacy, getting away - just the two of you, spending a day together, bed-and-breakfast getaways. Surprise one another again. Go for a walk in the park, begin to hold hands again. Find time for one another. Do spontaneous things, such as plan a date night. You can say something like, "I would like to take you somewhere this afternoon. I want to show you how much I love you." Then drive your spouse to the lake or beach and have someone go before you to set up a romantic picnic table with flowers and nice place settings. They could even place a blanket on the grass with a cooler containing fresh fruit, cheese, and champagne (non-alcoholic) on ice. Have some music that you and your partner once danced to playing in the background. Begin to talk about what happened when you first met.

Five Ways to Reconnect with your Spouse:

1. Daily touch, shoulder massage, a soft rub across the arm. Don't go to bed without touching your spouse a couple of times during the day.
2. Listen to your spouse; make eye contact.
3. Lay in bed to talk about life together - revive memories.
4. Make new memories; do something new together.
5. Improve Communication - Speak more kindly and be polite to one another.

Marriage Retreat

Another way to reconnect with your mate is to find, research, and book a marriage retreat package. They usually take place in a private, quiet, and beautiful setting. In this type of environment, you and your spouse will receive personalized attention, which will allow an in-depth focus on concerns and situations that need additional care, providing restoration and improvement in your relationship. Retreats may include lectures, discussions, role play, and interactions with other couples as well. It may allow time to step away from everyday life and focus on each other without outside distractions and noise.

Generally, retreats allow the time and place of spiritual refreshing and renewal. Marriage retreats may do the same, but they also serve to create emotional healing that is tailor-made just for renewed unity between you and your spouse. It also provides confidence and assurance that you are not alone in the marital challenges you currently face.

The warm, cozy atmosphere immediately puts you at ease. The comfort of this peaceful environment helps you fully unwind and enjoy the quality time you're spending together. A couples retreat may be the very thing to re-ignite the flames of your marriage again. This time away can help to restore passion and cause a fresh breeze of love to your relationship. Maybe even a weekend getaway together can cause a new beginning to awaken in your relationship. Create a new chapter of love and friendship to your marriage union by taking the time out to rediscover one another.

For some, it may be so easy to live together and to get along. Everything just lines up perfectly together in harmony in your relationship. Whereas in another relationship, there may be more struggle. I have found out that everyone has something to go through or has a cross to bear. My cross may be different from yours, but all in all, we must be diligent in maintaining cohesiveness in our marital relationships. We must purposely preserve unity at all times.

Psalms 133:1,2 (NKJV)
Behold, how good and how pleasant it is
For brethren to dwell together in unity!
It is like the precious oil upon the head,
Running down on the beard,
The beard of Aaron,
Running down on the edge of his garments.

Living in unity brings strength and power, which represents a bond that is not easily broken. Unity symbolizes stability and oneness with man and God. With unity comes the blessing of God, and the oil running down Aaron's beard represents God's presence, abundance, and blessing.

Jerome and I recognized that as we became closer in our relationship, blessings began to appear. We are happy, encouraged, and filled with joy and peace. These are the things that can't be purchased. These things come only from the Lord. Being content and on one accord in unity in your home is one of the greatest things we can ask for.

No matter what has happened in your marriage, God has the power to heal it. There is no failure in Him. Your marriage is capable of being restored. Jesus laid down His life for us. You may be the only way for your partner to see God. Call on Him and ask Him to forgive you of your sins. Ask Jesus to come into your heart, to live in you, and to be your savior and Lord. He is waiting on you. Jesus said:

John 14:14 (NIV)

"You may ask me for anything in my name, and I will do it."

I thank God that we no longer have to live as strangers in our house. No more strife and discontentedness, hurt, and unforgiveness.

Once you have asked the Lord to forgive you of all your sins and come into your heart, as your Savior and Lord, ask that you be filled with His Holy Spirit. Then instantly, you are forgiven. Now you are equipped to pray, fast, and intercede on behalf of your spouse and others.

I am a living witness; my husband would not bend or change in any way. He even confessed out of his mouth that he wouldn't change or repent and give his life to the Lord. He believed the lies of the devil but look at him now; he is free. He sings and lifts his hands in praise to worship God. Jerome confessed Jesus Christ as his Lord. He now attends church service. Many times when he is off work, he participates in our family bible study and expounds on the meaning of the scripture verses.

It was not an easy road, but God heard my prayers, and the Lord continued to work on Jerome as I lived a righteous life before him. I never wavered from trying to live in right standing with the Lord. The mountain of division in our home had to move. As I read the scriptures in the word of God to him and fasted at times, I began to see change. The mountain began to chip away. Whatever I saw that was not what I wanted to see, I would apply the word of God to and pray that every obstacle was moved.

There were times my husband would come to me and say, have you been praying for me? He didn't see or hear me praying for him; he just knew that I was.
Prayer was my way of asking the Father to open new doors to forgiveness and healing of our relationship from so many obstacles. Prayer is communicating with God. It is a time when you can go into your secret place: just you and the Father. Whatever you discuss with Him, you know that it will not be shared. Believe that whatever you ask for in prayer will manifest or come to pass.

I confess that my prayers were answered even before I saw it happen. For example, I would say thank you, Father God, for allowing Jerome and my tongues to be in agreement to do the service of the Lord. Father, I thank you for Jerome giving his whole heart to you. Thank you, Lord, for Jerome and I going to church together on Sundays. These and other daily prayer confessions were made over seasons of time until they came to pass. Now, Father God, Jesus your son said:

Mark 11:24 (NKJV)

Whatever things you ask for when you pray, believe that you receive them and you will have them.

We can now say that most of our spiritual high mountains have been made low. I write this because God is not through with my husband and me yet.

We are so very grateful. Now we can sing and praise the Lord on one accord, giving God the glory for all He has done in our lives and the lives of our family members.

How this writing assignment all began.

During a trip to Indianapolis, IN, to visit my daughter Patrice, we decided to go for a walk around her apartment complex to get some extra steps in. As we were sharing with one another, the question I asked Patrice was, "In five years, what do you see yourself doing?"
She, in turn, asked me what I could see myself doing in five years.
I replied, "Hopefully retiring by then." I said I would write a book if I had something to write about.

Several months later, while listening to some anointed praise music by Travis Greene and William McDowell, I began to worship before the Lord to several songs. While worshiping in the dance, I heard the heavenly Father say, "I need you to write a book called Husband of a Praying Wife." I was so elated and grateful that He would choose me for such an assignment. I must say, the Lord has been my help and guide in the writing of this lovely book. In writing it, I sincerely hope that many marriages will be completely restored and made whole.

References

1. Copeland, Germaine. Prayers That Avail Much. Volume 3, 1996, May, page 58.

2. Merriam-Webster. (n.d.). Encourage. In *Merriam-Webster.com thesaurus*. Retrieved March 12, 2022, from **https://www.merriam-webster.com/thesaurus/encourage**

3. Merriam-Webster. (n.d.). Forgive. In *Merriam-Webster.com dictionary*. Retrieved March 12, 2022, from **https://www.merriam-webster.com/dictionary/forgive**

4. Merriam-Webster. (n.d.). Hope. In *Merriam-Webster.com dictionary*. Retrieved March 12, 2022, from **https://www.merriam-webster.com/dictionary/hope**

5. Merriam-Webster. (n.d.). Intercession. In *Merriam-Webster.com dictionary*. Retrieved March 12, 2022, from **https://www.merriam-webster.com/dictionary/intercession**

Prayer Changes Things!!!

It is my sincere prayer that for every marriage that is struggling due to your spouse receiving salvation or any other problem, you will invite Father God to come in and fix it through the power of prayer, fasting, intercession, and the word of God spoken in faith. God hears your cry, and He will deliver. Again, I say, "There is nothing too hard for God!"

Minister Lisa M. Harris

I'd like to hear from you, contact me by email at: lisamarie.books01@gmail.com

Made in the USA
Columbia, SC
23 January 2023

10938098R10067